Tiny Readers
BIBLE
STORIES

Published by Candle Books
an imprint of
Lion Hudson plc
Wilkinson House, Jordan Hill Road,
Oxford OX2 8DR, England
www.lionhudson.com/candle

ISBN 978 1 78128 305 9
e-ISBN 978 1 78128 338 7

First edition 2016
The stories in this book were first published in the UK in 2011 and 2012
as the Tiny Readers board book collection

A catalogue record for this book is available from the British Library

Printed and bound in China, August 2016, LH17

Tiny Readers
BIBLE
STORIES

Karen Williamson
illustrated by Hannah Wood

CANDLE
BOOKS

Contents

Noah and the Great Flood

One day God told Noah, "You must build a great boat. It's going to rain like it's never rained before."

So Noah and his family began to build a huge boat. They sawed. They hammered. They painted.

At last the boat was finished.
Noah called it his "ark".

Now God told Noah, "Collect up two of every sort of animal." So Noah and his family gathered all the animals.

When the animals were ready,
Noah led them into the ark.

Now it started to rain. It poured, and poured, and poured! In no time, the boat was floating on the water.

But Noah, his family, and all the animals were safe inside the boat.

14

God was protecting them.

Finally, after many, many days,
the rain stopped.

Noah sent a raven flying across the water. But it never returned.

Next Noah sent a dove
flying across the water.

She flew back, carrying a leaf in her beak. She had found land.

At last the ark landed on a mountain.
Noah, his family, and all the animals
streamed out.

"See the wonderful rainbow!" God said.
"It is a sign that I love you."

Joseph and His Brothers

Jacob had twelve sons. He loved them all. But he loved Joseph more than the rest.

One day Jacob gave Joseph a special coat. His brothers were jealous. Why did Joseph get all the best things?

"I dreamt we each had a bundle of grain," Joseph told his brothers. "Your bundles all bowed down to mine."

"Do you think we will bow down to you?"
his brothers asked crossly. "You're not
king over us!"

One day Jacob said to Joseph,
"Take some food to your brothers –
they're away minding the sheep."

His brothers saw traders passing.
"Let's sell Joseph!" they said.

The traders took Joseph to Egypt,
where a rich man bought him.
Joseph worked hard for this man.

27

But the man's wife told lies about Joseph, and he was thrown into prison.

The king's servant was also in prison. One night he had a strange dream. "It means the king wants you to go back and work for him again," Joseph explained.

One night the king had peculiar dreams.

"I saw seven fat cows come out of the river," he said. "Then seven skinny cows swallowed the fat ones.

"Then I dreamt seven bad ears of grain swallowed seven good ears. What do these dreams mean?"

No one knew.

Suddenly the King's servant
remembered his friend Joseph.
"Bring him here now!" ordered the King.

32

The King told Joseph his dreams.
"Both dreams mean the same
thing," said Joseph.

"There will be seven good harvests –
then seven years with no harvest."

"God sent these dreams to warn you,"
Joseph told the King. "In the seven
hungry years, there will be no food.
Store the harvest in the good years,
then you can feed all your people in
the seven bad years."

So the king made Joseph his top man,
in charge of storing the harvest.
When the seven hungry years came,
everyone had enough to eat.

In the hungry time,
Jacob and his family
couldn't get any grain.
"Go to Egypt and buy grain,"
Jacob told his sons.

When they came to
Egypt, Joseph
saw that his
brothers had changed.
They were no longer cruel.

36

"I'm Joseph, your brother!" he told them. "You once sold me. Now hurry home and bring Father here to Egypt."

This is how God's people, the Israelites, came to live in Egypt.

The Princess and the Baby

There was once a wicked king of Egypt.

"There are far too many Israelites!"
he said. "Throw every Israelite baby
boy in the river."

One mother hid her baby at home.
But she was worried that a soldier
might hear him crying.

So she wove a basket out of reeds.
Then she painted it with tar to keep
out water.

Finally she put her baby in the basket
and floated it on the river.
"Hide here and watch what happens,"
she told her daughter, Miriam.

After a time, Miriam heard voices.
The princess was coming to bathe.

The princess saw the basket
in the reeds.

"Please bring it here!" she said.

43

"A beautiful baby!" gasped the princess. "I do wish he were mine."

Miriam crept up. "Do you need
someone to look after the baby?"
she asked.
"Yes please!" said the princess.
"Can you find me a helper?"

Miriam ran home.
"The princess found baby," she said.
"Now she wants a nurse for him."
Miriam's mother hurried to the river.

"I could nurse the baby," she said.
"Please do!" smiled the princess,
"When he's older, I'll make him my
own son."

The mother was so happy! Now her
baby could grow up safely at home.

Later she took her boy to the palace.

The princess said, "I will name him 'Moses' – it means 'taken from the water'."

God took care of young Moses.

Jonah and the Great Big Fish

One day God said to Jonah: "Go to the city of Nineveh! Tell the people there they have done wrong."

But Jonah was scared and ran away.
Jonah jumped on a ship that took him
far away from Nineveh.

God sent a great storm.
Waves splashed over the ship.
The sailors felt very scared.

Jonah lay asleep below deck.
"Wake up, Jonah!" called the captain.
"Help us – or we'll all drown!"

"I'm running away from God," said
Jonah. "That's why he sent this storm.
Throw me in the sea and it will stop!"

The moment Jonah hit the water, the storm stopped. Down into the swirling sea he sank.

Then, gulp! Something swallowed him.

It was a huge, huge fish!

Jonah was inside that fish for three days. "Help me, Lord!" he prayed.

At last the fish spat Jonah out on to a beach. Splasshh!

"Now go to Nineveh!" God said. "Tell the people they have done wrong." This time Jonah went to Nineveh to warn the people, as God told him.

The First Christmas

Mary and Joseph had to travel to Bethlehem. Mary was expecting her baby very soon.

The kind innkeeper let Mary and Joseph sleep in his stable.

"Baby Jesus is born in Bethlehem tonight," the angel told some startled shepherds.

61

The shepherds rushed off to find the newborn baby.

They soon found baby Jesus in the stable.

Wise men followed a bright star to find
Jesus. They journeyed many miles.

When they found little Jesus, they knelt down. They gave him rich presents.

The Boy Who Gave His Lunch

One day Jesus went to the hills for a rest. But crowds of people followed. Jesus told them some of his wonderful stories.

The day went on, and the sun began to set. People felt tired and very hungry.

"Shall we send them away to buy bread?" asked Jesus' friends.
"No – we must feed them," said Jesus.
"Does anyone here have food?"

"Has anyone brought food?" asked Jesus' friends. Everybody shook their heads.

Then a young boy said, "I have five little loaves and two small fish. Jesus can have them all."

The man brought the boy to Jesus.
"This boy has a few loaves and fish,"
he said.

Jesus smiled and took the boy's food.
"Ask everyone to sit down," he said.

Jesus took the loaves and broke them.
His friends gave out the food to people.
Jesus went on and on, giving out the
bread and fish.

There were more than five thousand people – and everyone had enough to eat.

Jesus' friends picked up the leftovers.
"Twelve baskets of scraps," said the
boy. "I brought just one basket of food.
This is a really great miracle!"

Jesus Stops a Storm

Jesus was with his special friends beside the lake.

Many people had come to listen to his wonderful stories.

The sun was now setting.
Jesus said, "Let's sail across to the
other side of the lake."

Jesus felt tired. He'd been talking to people all day. Soon he was fast asleep.

Suddenly a fierce wind sprang up.
Rain began to fall. The boat started to
rock. High waves splashed all around.

The sea tossed the boat to and fro.
It began to fill with water.

Jesus' friends felt very frightened.
But Jesus was still sleeping peacefully.

"Master, wake up!" they shouted.
"Help us – or we're going to drown!"

Jesus woke and stood up in the boat.
"Be still!" he ordered the storm.

The wind dropped. The rain stopped.
The waves vanished. All was still.

"Why were you so scared?" Jesus asked. "I am with you. You can always trust me."

The Lost Sheep

Once Jesus told a story about a loving shepherd.

This shepherd had exactly 100 sheep.
Every morning the shepherd counted
his sheep carefully. One, two, three,
four... 97, 98, 99, 100.

One night the shepherd counted his
sheep as usual. One was missing!
"I must find my lost sheep," he said.

So the shepherd shut his ninety-nine sheep safely in their fold and set out to search for the missing sheep.

He crossed streams and climbed hills.
Then, feeling very tired, he stopped
and listened.

Yes! It was the "baa" of his lost sheep.
The shepherd pulled his sheep from
the bush where it had got caught.

He carried his sheep safely home.
Then he called to his friends.
"Be happy!" he said.
"I've found my
lost sheep!"

Jesus said, "I'm like a good shepherd. I care for people who get lost."

Jesus Meets Zacchaeus

In the town of Jericho lived a man called Zacchaeus. Nobody liked him.

Zacchaeus collected tax money from all the people.

But he took much more than he was
supposed to. He stole people's money.

"Zacchaeus is rich *because* he takes too much money from us," they moaned.

One day people heard Jesus was coming. They crowded the streets to see him. But Zacchaeus was so small he couldn't see a thing.

Suddenly Zacchaeus had a great idea! He climbed a tree and perched on a branch. Now he could *see* Jesus coming.

When Jesus reached the tree,
he stopped and looked up.
"Zacchaeus, come down!" Jesus
shouted. "I want to come to dinner
with you!"

Zacchaeus was astonished!
He slid down the tree and took
Jesus home.

Zacchaeus gave Jesus a great meal.
The two men talked late into the night.

After meeting Jesus, Zacchaeus gave back all the money he'd stolen.
"This is a special day for you." Jesus told him. "God is pleased with you."